100

W9-AHA-757

Wolves Have Pups

by Elizabeth Dana Jaffe

Animals and Their Young

Content Adviser: Janann Jenner, Ph.D.

Science Adviser: Terrence E. Young Jr., M.Ed., M.L.S.,
Jefferson Parish (La.) Public Schools

Reading Adviser: Dr. Linda D. Labbo,
Department of Reading Education, College of Education,
The University of Georgia

COMPASS POINT BOOKS

Minneapolis, Minnesota

Compass Point Books
3722 West 50th Street, #115
Minneapolis, MN 55410

Visit Compass Point Books on the Internet at *www.compasspointbooks.com* or e-mail your request to
custserv@compasspointbooks.com

Photographs ©: Richard Day/Daybreak Imagery cover; Robert McCaw 4, 20; Thomas Kitchin/Tom Stack &
Associates 6; Tom Walker/Visuals Unlimited 8; Tom & Therisa Stack/Tom Stack & Associates 10; Warren K.
Williams/Visuals Unlimited 12; Jane McAlonan/Visuals Unlimited 14; Joe McDonald/McDonald Wildlife
Photography 16, 18.

Editors: E. Russell Primm, Emily J. Dolbear, and Laura Driscoll
Photo Researchers: Svetlana Zhurkina and Jo Miller
Photo Selector: Linda S. Koutris
Designer: Bradfordesign, Inc.

Library of Congress Cataloging-in-Publication Data

Jaffe, Elizabeth Dana.
     Wolves have pups / by Elizabeth D. Jaffe.
        p. cm. — (Animals and their young)
     Includes bibliographical references (p.   ).
     Summary: Describes the birth, growth, development, and reproduction of wolves.
     ISBN 0-7565-0171-7 (hardcover)
        1. Wolves—Infancy—Juvenile literature. [1. Wolves. 2. Animals—Infancy.] I. Title. II. Series.
QL737.C22 J34 200
599.773—dc21   2001004134

Table of Contents

What Are Wolf Pups?

Baby wolves are called **wolf pups**. Wolves are related to dogs. Wolves are like dogs in some ways. They are both smart and playful with one another. But wolves are wild animals.

In the wild, wolves live in groups called **packs**. Every wolf pack has two leaders. One leader is male. The other is female. In most packs, the two leaders are the only wolves that have young.

What Happens Before Wolf Pups Are Born?

The mother wolf has her pups in the spring. The wolf pups grow inside the mother for about 63 days.

Then the mother wolf goes into the **den**. This is where the pups are born. Most mother wolves give birth to four to six pups at one time.

A mother wolf looks out of her den.

What Happens After Wolf Pups Are Born?

Wolf pups are born with their eyes closed. They cannot see or hear. They are very small. Each pup is 8 to 9 inches (20 to 23 centimeters) long.

The wolf pups stay inside the den with their mother for a few weeks. She makes sure they are fed, clean, and safe.

After two weeks, the wolf pups open their eyes. Then they begin to walk.

How Do Wolf Pups Feed?

Newborn wolf pups **nurse**, or drink milk from their mother. Milk is the only food they get for the first few weeks.

Meanwhile, the other wolves in the pack go hunting. They bring food to the mother in the den. She must keep her body strong. Her body can then make more milk for her babies.

Wolf pups drink milk from their mother.

What Does a Wolf Pup Look Like?

A wolf pup looks a lot like a puppy dog. Its body is covered with short fur. It has four legs and a little tail. Its ears are floppy, and its nose is short and flat.

A wolf pup's front paws are bigger than its back paws. Each front paw has five toes. Each back paw has four toes.

◀ A wolf pup looks a lot like a puppy dog, but it is a wild animal.

What Colors Are Wolf Pups?

Most wolf pups are the same color as their parents. They may be white, black, yellow, gray, brown, red, or a mix of all these colors.

Wolf pups are born with blue eyes. Their eyes become deep yellow when they are older.

What Do Wolf Pups Do and Eat?

Three- or four-week-old wolf pups come out of the den. They love to run around and play. They push, chase, and nip one another. These games help the pups learn hunting skills. They will use these skills when they grow up.

The pups continue to drink their mother's milk. They also start to eat meat. Wolves mostly eat meat. They hunt deer, beavers, fish, moose, and other animals.

What Happens As a Wolf Pup Grows Older?

A wolf pup's fur gets thicker as the pup grows. Its tail and its back legs get longer. Its ears stand up straight on its head. When it is six months old, a wolf pup is almost as big as an adult wolf. It is strong enough to go on a hunt.

Wolf pups use their ears, tails, and faces to show how they feel. They also make noises. They bark, growl, whimper, and howl at one another.

Pups make noises when they play.

When Is a Wolf Pup Grown-up?

A nine-month-old wolf pup is fully grown. An adult wolf can be 6 feet (1.8 meters) long or more.

Some wolves leave the pack before they are two years old. They go off to find mates. They will have pups of their own. They start new wolf packs. In the wild, most wolves live to be five to eight years old.

At one time, wolves were found in many parts of the world. Sadly, large numbers of them have been killed. Today wolves are an endangered animal in most areas. Scientists are working hard to protect them.

◀ A pack of gray wolves

Glossary

den—a cave or hole where wolf pups are born and raised

nurse—to drink milk produced by the mother

packs—groups of wolves that live and hunt together

wolf pups—baby wolves

Did You Know?

- Wolf pups learn the smell of their mother and their brothers and sisters before they can see.

- Wolves can hear a sound from 3 or 4 miles (4.8 to 6.4 kilometers) away.

- Wolves are great runners. They can keep up a steady pace for many hours. In a sprint, they can run as fast as 40 miles (64 kilometers) per hour.

Want to Know More?

At the Library

Gibbons, Gail. *Wolves*. New York: Holiday House, 1994.

Lepthien, Emilie U. *Wolves*. Chicago: Childrens Press, 1991.

Simon, Seymour. *Wolves*. New York: HarperCollins Publishers, 1993.

On the Web

International Wolf Center: Pup Page

http://www.wolf.org/pup/index.htm

For photos of wolf pups born at the International Wolf Center in Ely, Minnesota

Wild Sentry

http://www.bitterroot.net/wild/

For information on how your teacher can invite a real wolf to visit your classroom

Through the Mail

KLAW Club Newsletter

c/o The Richard E. Flauto Wildlife Foundation

P.O. Box 9452

Youngstown, OH 44513

To order a newsletter about wolves, written by kids for kids

On the Road

Wolf Park

4012 East 800 North

Battle Ground, IN 47920

765/567-2265

To get an up-close look at several packs of gray wolves; open from May to November

Index

About the Author
After graduating from Brown University, Elizabeth Dana Jaffe received her master's degree in early education from Bank Street College of Education. Since then, she has written and edited educational materials. Elizabeth Dana Jaffe lives in New York City.

Cherokee IRC